Pearls of Knowledge

Advice from the 'Ulema

Written and Compiled by:
Sheikh Mateen Charbonneau

Publisher: Household Publications
Date of Publication: 10/18/2023
Pages: 83

I DEDICATE THE REWARD OF THIS BOOK TO IMAM SAJJAD
(PEACE BE UPON HIM)

Table of Contents

Ayatollah Sayyid Mohammad Taqi al-Modarresi issued a letter to Universal Muslims Association of America 2018 7

Advice on how to get closer to Imam Mahdi (aj) - Sayyid Murtadha Shirazi Arbaeen 2012 15

Advice from Sheikh Rafati - Arbaeen 2015 16

General Advice from Ayatollah Sayyid Murtadha Shirazi- 2019 19

Advice from Ayatollah Murtaza Mutahhari 21

Advice from Ayatollah Sayyid Muhammad Taqi al-Modarresi about seeking and retaining knowledge- 2019 24

Advice from Ayatollah Muhammad Hussain Mujahid -2019 25

Advice from Ayatollah Naser Makarem Shirazi .. 27

Advice from Sheikh Jafar Rafati for tabligh (communicating the message of Islam) 29

Advice for tabligh from Sayyid Murtadha Shirazi (communicating the message of Islam) -2016 30

Advice from Ayatollah Sayyid Taqi Modaressi for doing tabligh (communicating the message of Islam) - 2018 31

Advice from Sayyid Abdul Husayn Dastghaib Shirazi 33

General Advice from Sayyid Murtadha Shirazi - 2015 37

The guidance for orators on the advent of the month of Muharram by Ayatollah Sayyid Ali Al-Sistani 38

The late Sayyid Muhammad al-Shirazi's advice to the representatives of the Maraji' about Time Management 44

Advice of Ayatollah Sheikh Ishaq Fayyadh about Interacting with others -2019 46

Advice of Ayatollah Sayyid Murtadha Shirazi about Quality and Quantity- 2019 48

Advice of Ayatollah Sheikh Ishaq Fayyadh about students of knowledge -2019 54

Advice of Ayatollah Sayyid Murtadha Shirazi for the Students of Knowledge – 2019 55

Advice from Sheikh Abdul-Karim al-Haeri about Mercy 59

Advice from Ayatollah Sayyid Muhammad Ridha Shirazi about Participating in the Rituals of Imam Hussain (a) 65

Advice of Ayatollah Sayyid Sadiq Shirazi about hope, decision making and facing problems 83

Ayatollah Sayyid Mohammad Taqi al-Modarresi issued a letter to Universal Muslims Association of America 2018

The letter of the Grand Ayatollah Sayyid Mohammad Taqi al-Modarresi is as follows:

In the name of God, Most Gracious, Most Merciful

Respected scholars and community leaders, civic and political activists, honorable guests and attendees of the Universal Muslims Association of America, As-Salamu Alaykum.

From the Islamic seminary in the Holy City of Karbala I send you greetings of peace and prayers for prosperity. I also send you the blessings of Imam Hussain (a), a man who stood up for the cause of justice, freedom, and godly principles and became a legendary martyr in that cause. A man who treated his dear son the same loving way as the black Christian servant who died defending Hussain (a). His majestic shrine here in the holy city of Karbala is thus the focal point of over twenty million people who participate in the biggest annual pilgrimage known as Arbaeen.

The world is now a global village and communities are more connected than ever before. No matter how many walls we build, there will always be more bridges that connect us. For better or worse, we are all in the same boat. So, we need a clear vision for the future and robust theories that help tackle our common challenges.

To Muslims in America, I say, first, we must ask; who are we? Are we aliens living in a foreign land? Or are we part and parcel of this nation? Do we abandon our identity? Or do we remain attached to our home countries? Do we engage in the internal affairs of those far away regions and live in isolation, shielding ourselves from the host culture, or we do adopt this country as our permanent abode?

The Prophet (s) has famously said, خير الأوطان ما حملك. Meaning, the best home is the one that provides for you.

And since this country has provided for you opportunities not afforded to you elsewhere, then you must believe that it will forever be your home.

But what about our religion and the big role it plays in our lives? Do we hold on to everything in it as it is practiced in Muslim countries? What about certain rites and rituals which may be unsuited to this environment? These are questions we must address or risk losing our identity and values.

For most people, religion has been meshed with culture and while culture has its value, it is separate from religion. While culture is subject to change, faith is divine and sublime.

Even within the framework of religion, we must define priorities and make a distinction between what is important and what is more important. Thus, we can prioritize and if must be, sacrifice the lesser for the greater. In short, there are rules, then there are cardinal rules.

One narration states: من اشتغل بالمهم ضيَّع الأهم *"Whoever gets occupied by things that are important, will risk losing that which is more important."*

Between these two is a very fine and delicate line, because every country has its own unique conditions and evolving norms, but jurists have the ability to do so – with God's help.

Focusing on the family unit, education, and community is key. We must empower our women and provide them with every resource to take their rightful position as not passive participants, but leaders in our common struggles, seeking inspiration from lives of such legendary heroines as Lady Zainab (a) who challenged the vilest tyrant of her day, shaking his throne and destroying his evil empire with little more than her voice.

Not only should we promote the value of community gatherings on Fridays and Eid's, but to galvanize community members for positive social, economic, and political change. You must participate in public life and be good citizens. We must foster cooperation at every level, helping those in lower socio-economic stages to reach higher and become productive members of society.

We must work toward establishing religious seminaries in the United States, which would produce indigenous faith leaders and – in the long term – even jurists (Maraje'a) who can crystallize a vision of the future compatible with the community's needs and unique qualities. These scholars would maintain a close tie with their counterparts in the major seminaries and bring the world of religious scholarship to a modern western context.

In short, I explore the Muslim community to strive for positive integration on all levels of life in the United States; culturally, politically, and economically while maintaining our values and faith traditions, in line with the teachings and examples of the Ahl ul Bayt (a).

You must engage with the wider community; your neighbors, co-workers, classmates are members of the human family. Instead of being an indignant minority, lead the charge to improving the lives of everyone around you and making a positive change.

Prophets and divinely appointed apostles never came with the intent of ruling over people, but to serve them with social justice. Even when they did reach positions of authority, they refused to use those positions for personal gain. When he was chosen as leader of fifty of today's countries, stretching from Morocco in the Western tip of Africa, to the Russian republic of Dagestan in the heart of Asia, in what was a global superpower that had defeated both the Roman and Persian empires, Imam Ali (a), moved from his native city of Madinah to the capital city of Kufa. In his first public address as ruler, he said that *"I have come here with only two shirts and my mule. If, at the end of my tenure I leave you with anything more than that, then I have betrayed you and that I will never do."*

He also instructed his governors to listen to the people, consult them on policy matters, and treat everyone with justice and equity irrespective of race or creed, famously declaring the statement now etched across history; *"People are of two types; either your brothers in faith, or your equals in humanity."*

He refused to have bodyguards, making himself accessible to everyone. A Jewish man once came to Medina seeking an audience with the ruler. To his surprise, he was pointed in the direction of a man resting under a tree. No bodyguards, no security detail, just an old man lying in the shadow of a date palm! Astonished, the man said to Imam Ali (a); your justice is your security and why don't you have any fear of being assassinated? He had enemies, as you would if you so radically sought to challenge the status quo, enemies who would insult him to his face, but he let them be, so long as he was their sole target and the citizens were safe.

But perhaps the most notable aspect of Imam Ali's (a) system of government was his unwavering commitment to the poor, the voiceless, the minorities. He lived the life of the poorest of his citizens so he could empathize with them and not be swayed by the hypnotizing allure of power and money. *"Gold and silver should find another to deceive", he would declare. "This authority that I've got is more worthless to me than the mucus of a sneezing goat, unless I can use it to restore justice for those oppressed."*

It is these legendary stories of moral courage that have immortalized Imam Ali (a) such that we continue to be inspired by him 1,400 years after his passing.

In a toxic climate characterized by ignorance and intolerance, the world needs examples like his and more leaders willing to resist egoistic temptations and upholding universal values of justice, compassion, love, and equity for all.

Advice on how to get closer to Imam Mahdi (aj) - Sayyid Murtadha Shirazi Arbaeen 2012

I asked Sayyid Murtadha Shirazi to give us some advice on how to get closer to our 12th Imam (aj). The first thing he replied was that this is an easy thing to say, but in reality, it is not an easy task to accomplish. He continued to say that we needed to pray to Allah and ask Him to open our container and expand our capacity, so that we can receive the knowledge pertaining to Imam Mahdi (aj). For example, a 12oz cup can only hold 12oz of water. No matter how much water you pour into that cup it will only hold 12oz. However, if we have a larger container we will have the capacity to hold more.

Being among those who are close to the Imam means having a very high level of knowledge and piety, so we must be prepared mentally and spiritually to understand, comprehend, and accept this knowledge.

He proceeded to say that one of the ways that we can gain proximity to the Imam (aj) is to fulfill all of our obligations (*wajibat*) that Allah has asked from us.

Next is to stay away from all of the things Allah has forbidden us from doing (*muharramat*). This reminds me of the first thing he told me when he said that it sounded easy but in reality, was not an easy task at all. Last of all he told me that to become close to the Imam we should be careful of how we treat others. We should always treat others well, with respect and give them their due rights. We should never be oppressors and mistreat people.[1]

---

[1] Relayed by Sheikh Mateen Charbonneau

Advice from Sheikh Rafati - Arbaeen 2015

He said to me: Don't rush for preaching and focus on studying to attain the highest level. He said to make the intention of guiding one million or more people. He said it may seem unattainable for one person to do, but it is possible and gave me the example of Sheikh Zakzaky in Nigeria. He said that even if I died before beginning to preach, I will be rewarded for preaching all those years and for all the goals I had such as guiding that amount of people.

He said while I was blessed to be in Karbala for Ziyarat Arbaeen to ask Imam Hussain (a) to help me because Allah gave him power to do miraculous things. For example, if he wanted, he could turn a man to an angel and a rock into gold. He said the visitor has a right upon the one visited and that is to answer him, help him and provide the things requested.[2]

---

[2] Relayed by Sheikh Mateen Charbonneau

General Advice from Ayatollah Sayyid Murtadha Shirazi- 2019

Ahl ul Bayt (a) are the top of the creation so whatever we should do as Shia should be the best. We should be the best in the field we go into. We shouldn't be content with our current situation, but should try to set higher goals for ourselves.

Rush towards these goals:

1. Expanding our knowledge everyday
2. We should have good actions not just in quantity but in quality
3. To obtain *taqwa* (God-conciousness) and always remember Allah
4. We should improve our *akhlaq* (morality) by comparing ourselves with our past. We should always strive to improve.
5. Enjoin good and forbid evil by finding various new methods. Evil is being spread continuously in many new ways, so we must find new and creative ways to spread goodness to people.[3]

---

[3] Relayed by Sheikh Mateen Charbonneau

Advice from Ayatollah Murtaza Mutahhari

A human being must rely on his own conduct and personal initiative. What is more explicit than the phrase of the Qur'an which says: *"There is not for man save what he strives for."* Quran 53:39, No doubt, it involves human dynamism, alertness, insight and ability.

Today, educators try hard to awaken the sense of self-reliance in man, and rightly do so. The kind of self-reliance that Islam awakens in man is that it puts an end to the hope of relying on everything outside himself, and if there is a hope it must be centered on oneself. Similarly, every connection with other things or persons is through action. You cannot be connected with the Prophet (s) or Imam Ali (a) or the latter's chaste wife Fatima (a) except through deeds.

I remember a narration from eighteen years ago which affected me deeply. It was an anecdote from the life of the Holy Prophet (s), so fine and meaningful, and peerless in the biography of all human beings. It is amazing how a man in a desert environment, such as that of the Prophet's could act in an extraordinarily thoughtful manner.

The Prophet (s) on one of his travels with his companions ordered the caravan to stop and dismount. Then he dismounted and started walking in a certain direction. Soon he returned, and his companions thought that he was looking for a suitable place for camping before he could decide about moving to another spot. They saw him approach his camel, take a knee-band from the sack, tie the camel's knees and walk on as before. They wondered why the Prophet (s) had walked so far and back for such a trifling task and asked him why he did not order them to do it. The Prophet (s) said: *"Never seek help from others even for a small piece of work. Try to do it yourself."*

If the Prophet (s) had said this from the pulpit it would not have had such a deep effect, but he said it when it was combined with action. My purpose is to show that one of the principles of Islamic teachings which revive Islamic thought is action and reliance on action."[4]

---

[4] Reviving Islamic Ethos, A Compendium of Five Lectures Murtadha Mutahhari

Advice from Ayatollah Sayyid Muhammad Taqi al-Modarresi about seeking and retaining knowledge 2019

I asked the Sayyid what is some advice for seeking knowledge and retaining it. His reply was:

"When we go look for the moon, we spot it with our eyes and have certainty because we have searched for it and spotted it with our own eyes. This is more effective than someone just telling us that they saw the moon and us taking their word for it. When we want knowledge, we should go out and search for it ourselves then we would have certainty from seeing and learning this knowledge ourselves. We would be able to derive the knowledge from its sources, rather than just relying on what people say.

When we learn knowledge, we should teach it to others. In this way it will stay fresh with us and we are also benefiting others. When you learn knowledge, you gain one amount of knowledge but when you teach it you gain multiple times.

We should focus on memorizing Quran as this is very beneficial, but also helps our memory in all other aspects of retaining knowledge."[5]

---

[5] Relayed by Sheikh Mateen Charbonneau

Advice from Ayatollah Muhammad Hussain Mujahid 2019

While staying in our dorm room at the howza in Najaf, we saw an older Afghan gentleman walking in the hall and we gave him salam. We had no idea who he was as he did not have his religious attire on at the moment. He started talking with us and we invited him in our room for breakfast. He turned out to be a student of Grand Ayatollah Sayyid Khoei (r) and other great maraja. He had reached the level of *Ijtihad* many years ago and does many great things in Afghanistan and Quetta, Pakistan. We asked him to give us some advice for being good students and reaching the higher levels of knowledge.

The Ayatollah said: "Whatever you do trust in Allah. Next do *Tawassul* of the Imam's (a). We also must trust in our Imams (a). Why? Because Ahl ul Bayt (a) know our actions. We have narrations that our actions get reported to them Mondays and Thursdays. They know about our works and our situation. We should make sure we are in a good position with our actions.

Then he started telling us this story: A person named Dawud who was a companion of Imam Sadiq (a) had a cousin who was from the Ahl ul Sunnah. Dawud wanted to go to hajj. His cousin had a bad relationship with him but also needed some money for his daily needs. Dawud said even though he is bad with me I am still going to give him some money without telling anyone.

He then goes to Imam Sadiq (a) and before Dawud starts speaking any word to the Imam (a) the Imam says: Dawud you did a very great action to your cousin. Dawud says what action are you referring to? The Imam said that you gave some money to your cousin and it made me very happy and it shows that you are a good person. He asked how he came to know this, because he didn't tell anyone not even his wife? The Imam (a) said: Don't you know that all your deeds and actions are reported to the Imam of the time, from Allah, on Mondays and Thursdays.

He asked that we all take a picture together. After this he said his farewell to us then set off on foot towards Imam Hussain (a) as he does every year. He has been walking to Imam Hussain (a) every year in Arbaeen and also has been to Hajj 45 times.[6]

---

[6] Relayed by Sheikh Mateen Charbonneau

Advice from Ayatollah Naser Makarem Shirazi

مَنْ حَاوَلَ أَمْراً بِمَعْصِيَةِ اللهِ كانَ أَفْوَتُ لِما يَرجُو وَاَسْرَعُ لِما يَحْذِرُ

Imam al-Hussain (a) is narrated to have said: *"He who seeks to do something through sinning against God will lose what he hopes for sooner and reach what he feared for more quickly."*

"Some people imagine that they will reach their goals sooner if they resort to unlawful (Haram) means. For example, someone may be in a financial bind and they may think that by opening up a liquor store, they can save themselves from their financial problems and gain significant amounts of profit.

The aforementioned tradition has explicitly mentioned that this is not the case and in fact, they will become even further engulfed in various issues than before.

In other cases, some people may think that because they are constantly suffering from financial issues, once they make more money, they can finally gain a sense of inner peace and calm. They then imagine that the quickest way to make this money will be through various unlawful means. Once they have made this money, they realize that they have not gained any additional sense of peace and, in fact, they are more stressed out and anxious than ever before. This shows us that we should never seek what we need through unlawful means; such actions will only take us further away from our goals."[7]

---

[7] One Hundred and Fifty Life Lessons by Naser Makarem Shirazi Lesson 92

Advice from Sheikh Jafar Rafati for *tabligh* (communicating the message of Islam)

Constantly think of improving the situation of society to hasten the reappearance of the Imam (a) because *ghaybah* (occultation of the 12th Imam) is due to the sins of the people.

1. Make an organization under the Imam's name
2. Tell people about him and introduce him to them
3. Never think of yourself as low
4. Set a high goal for yourself so you reach that goal or at least something close to it

When you plant a seed, it takes some years to get the result: the fruit. So, things take time to see the fruit of your labor and you may not even see the results in this generation. Don't let this deter you from working in this noble cause and know that you are working towards building the foundation for greater things to come.[8]

---

[8] Relayed by Sheikh Mateen Charbonneau

Advice for *tabligh* from Sayyid Murtadha Shirazi (communicating the message of Islam) 2016

1. Recite *Ayatul Kursi* (3 *ayaat*) before ascending the mimbar (pulpit)
2. Find a few good capable people from the community to teach them so they can become scholars and teachers
3. Contact students of universities and also prominent people who will have a large impact on the masses.
4. The best of people are those who benefit the people the most (hadith). Be a servant of the people (Muslim and non-Muslim) in all aspects not just spiritual.
5. Have the best morals with people at all times.
6. Make nonprofit organization for defending the oppressed
7. Counseling those who have family problems
8. To get more sustenance keep good family relations and after fajr face the qibla, place your your right hand on your chest and say: *Yaa Fattah Yaa Razzaq* 70 times.[9]

---

[9] Relayed by Sheikh Mateen Charbonneau

Advice from Ayatollah Sayyid Taqi Modaressi for doing *tabligh* (communicating the message of Islam) 2018

Make pure intentions that every action you do is to please Allah and Allah will help you.

Don't attract people with money or power but with *Akhlaq* (morals) and *'ilm* (knowledge).

People don't see your knowledge, but they only see your *Akhlaq* (morality).

Akhlaq is like a beautiful apple which is attractive to those who see it. Once people approach you due to your *Akhlaq* it is as if they took the apple and bit into it thus opening the chance to show them your knowledge and guide them. However, if the outer appearance of the apple is rotten then people will never approach it to see what is inside.

Always behave with people in a good and forgiving way no matter who they are: Jews, Christians, Muslims, Non-Muslims or even Criminals, because they can always ask for forgiveness from Allah like in the example of Hurr the companion of Imam Hussain (a).[10]

---

[10] Relayed by Sheikh Mateen Charbonneau

Advice about the Holy Quran from Sayyid Abdul Husayn Dastghaib Shirazi

"Among Muslims there are people who receive the Holy Quran as a gift and then place it ceremoniously on a shelf or keep it with themselves as a means of protection. No doubt the use of the Holy Quran for such purposes is good and also an effective deed, but the problem is that the Quran has not come exclusively for such purposes; they are only secondary. It will be an insult to Quran if it is accepted that it was revealed only for such petty purposes.

Its example is like that of a man who gets an invitation from the king. That unwise fellow neither opens that royal letter not reads it. Even if he opens it, he only looks at the writing and even if he reads the words he does not know their meaning. He simply utters them orally. Even if he understands them, he gets no inspiration to see the king. He is not prepared to attend the royal court. He merely kisses the king's letter and then either puts it in his pocket or on a shelf in his house. In this way, has he not insulted the royal invitation? Will he not make the king frown at him for this behavior?

The condition of most of the Muslims is like this. Only a few keep any spirited connection with the Holy Quran. A majority of them, in order to get divine rewards are content with mere recitation of the words.

No doubt the Words of Allah are in themselves radiance and there is reward in merely reading, writing or even looking at them. But the original and main purpose of the revelation of the Holy Quran is that man must think over its verses so that his heart may turn towards the higher world. His heart may not entertain hopes from this world but become inclined towards the Hereafter. The study of Quranic verses makes the heart warm and then man becomes ever ready to act according to its commandments.

The Lord of the universe has ordered man to think and ponder at many places including the following, where He ordains: *"It is a Book We have revealed to you abounding in good that they may ponder over its verses, and that those endowed with understanding may be mindful." Quran 38:29*

Allah says about the effectiveness of the verses of Quran: *"Allah has revealed the best announcement, a book conformable in its various parts, repeating, whereat do shudder the skins of those who fear their*

Lord, then their skins and their hearts soften to the remembrance of Allah; this is Allah's guidance, He guides with it whom He pleases; and as for him whom Allah leaves to err, there is no guide for him." Quran 39:23

What is meant to convey is that the verses describing the punishment of the Hereafter make the reciter fearful and those promising mercy make the hearts happy and satisfied. Therefore if a man does not get affected by reciting Quran then know that he reads the Quran in a state of mind when both his heart and mind were involved in their love for the material world.

In his sermon, Amirul Momineen (a) says about the virtues of the pious people, *"These people recite the chapters of the Holy Quran with intense thought. They make their hearts melancholic by its recitation. They remedy their troubles and illnesses with the same verses of Quran. When they read verses relating to Divine Mercy their hearts incline to it with intense desire to get the same. When they hear verses mentioning Allah's chastisement, both their ears and hearts become so much attentive to them as if they hear the horrible roar of Hellfire."*

There are hundreds of verses in the Holy Quran wherein the punishments of the Hereafter as well as the niceties of Paradise have been detailed at length and then its followers have been invited to make this attainment the center of their efforts. It has also condemned worldly life and revealed its defects and drawbacks. Allah says: *And this life of the world is nothing but a sport and a play; and as for the next abode, that most surely is the life- did they but know!* Quran 29:64

In other words it is like the example of children gathering to play for a while and then disperse and return to their homes. The fact is that only the life of the Hereafter is the real and everlasting life.

Now the question which inevitably arises is, after reading and hearing all these verses, have the hearts of Muslims turned away from this world and inclined towards the Hereafter or they are mere orally and apparently expressing their belief in Quran and Islam while their thoughts and deeds, just like the materialists, have discarded the thought of the Hereafter altogether?"[11]

---

[11] Qalbe-Saleem, Immaculate Conscience by Sayyid Abdul Husayn Dastghaib Shirazi Chapter: Is Quran revealed as a Good Luck Charm

General Advice from Sayyid Murtadha Shirazi 2015

1. Make strong connection with Allah
2. Make connection with people by serving them
3. Use every moment to increase ones knowledge
4. Imam Ali (a) said: *"Anyone who makes a goal will reach that goal or something close to that."* Make an action plan to achieve those goals.
5. Get a small group of people together (10 for example) to help reach this goal and have a weekly program or meeting with them to come up with ideas on how to reach the goal.
6. Study: Sahifa Sajadiya, Al-Ihtijaj, and Nahjul Balagha[12]

---

[12] Relayed by Sheikh Mateen Charbonneau

The guidance for orators on the advent of the month of Muharram by Ayatollah Sayyid Ali Al-Sistani

Issued by Imam Ali (a) Foundation - London, the liaison office of His Eminence Ayatollah Sayyid Ali Al-Sistani on 23 Thi Alhija 1437

In the name of Allah the Gracious the Merciful and peace be on Mohammad and his pure progeny

"So, regarding religious ceremonies with the high respect reflects the hearts' devoutness."

The month of Muharram is approaching and we remember through it the greatest movement that had been led by reformists in the field of society's development, the awaking of the will of the nations and the restoration of circumstances. It is the blessed Hussaini Movement and to maintain this movement places on our shoulders- we, the followers of Imam Al-Hussain, a great responsibility which is the responsibility of preserving the continuity of this movement and strengthening its consequences and influences on the souls and hearts, and no Hussaini follower is without a sort of responsibility regardless to his position- a religious scholar, an educated individual or a specialist in one of the various fields of materialistic and human sciences. Every one of us has to shoulder the responsibility of preserving this blessed Hussaini uprising through the improvement of oneself, his family and the people around him and educating the individuals of his society by raising awareness of this uprising and the greatness of this Hussaini project.

However, orators bear the great duty because they represent the case and the project of Ashura uprising to the media. Therefore, we need to stop for a while and ask: Is the orator able to represent and perform this task in compliance to the needs of the time and the rising requirements of the modern age for achieving the Hussaini uprising blessed effects in the hearts and the souls?

Based on this point we must state some of the instructions and advice for anyone who wants to be a lecturer at the Hussaini gatherings.

1- The variety of the subjects to be tackled because society is in need for spiritual, educational and historical matters and this requires for the orator/lecturer to be well educated and prepared to have various subjects in many different fields which cover the needs of the attenders and others.

2-The orator/ lecturer must be well educated and a good pursuer of the issues of his age and this means he is able to realize and be aware of the ideological doubts arising in every sect and be able to read the changing behaviors in every society and at all times the believers come through because pursuing the new ideas, educational issues and behaviors would encourage people eager to attend the Hussaini gatherings as the ceremony becomes alive and influential on them.

3-The orator/ lecturer must be very vigilant in selecting the Quranic verses and relating the honest narrations from authentic references and mentioning the historical agreed on events because without verifying the sources of the narrations or the stated stories there may arise doubts about the effect of the authenticity of the *Al-Hussaini Mimbar* in the minds of the attendees.

4- *Al-Hussaini Mimbar* must not utilize dreams and untrue narrations which would defame its dignity, and would make it look as a cheap propaganda that is not compatible with the listeners' minds and their educational levels.

5-The good preparation means the orator/ lecturer has to be very vigilant and careful about the issues he talks about as preparation of the subject, its classification and dealing with it clearly in good style with the careful choice of attractive vocabulary for the attenders is very vital. If the orator/ lecturer spends a good amount of effort on preparing, classifying and exposing the issue in an eloquent and attractive method this would help the listeners to react to the *Al-Hussaini Mimbar*.

6- Ahl ul Bayt's heritage (a) is great and excellent, but the orator's/lecturer's skill and his creativity is clearly manifested in his choice of the texts and the traditions that form an attraction for all people regardless to their origins, religions, ideologies, in guidance with Ahl ul Bayt stress: *If people know the goodness of our language, they would have followed us.* The eloquence of their language is in their heritage that focuses on the human values which attract people from of different religions and various backgrounds.

7- Talking about the common well-known social problems and providing successful solutions to them. It is unlikely acceptable for the orator/lecturer to focus on exposing the issue only because exposing the issue of family collapse or its disintegration, for example, or the gap between the new generation and the older one or the divorce problem and other problems would allow fruitless discussions without the involvement of *Al-Hussaini Mimbar* in a positive way, and therefore, it is hoped that the orators/lecturers of the *Al-Hussaini Mimbar* consult those who are experts in social and educational fields such as psychologist and sociologists for assigning the right useful solutions for the social problems because dealing with the issue in this method would transfer *Al-Hussaini Mimbar* from the state of stagnancy to a state of leadership in the improvement of societies and setting them right.

8- *Al-Hussaini Mimbar* must be elevated higher than dealing with unsettled Shi'a issues regardless to their types because engaging in these issues would force *Al-Hussaini Mimbar* to favor one side on the other or cause a social chaos or may cause division among the believers while the *Al-Hussaini Mimbar* is a banner for the word unity and a symbol for Al-Hussain's light that gathers and attracts all those whom Hussain (a) is their favorite and who leads them to be on one path with active cooperation.

9- To give attention to common jurisprudence issues in the field of religious observances and the daily business relations by exposing and dealing with them in a charming plain style that makes the listener feel that *Al-Hussaini Mimbar* takes care of his/her reality and various issues.

10- To stress the importance of *Al-Marji'ya*[13] and scholarly *Hawza* (seminary) and the scholarly base that is behind the strength of the Twelver Sect (Imami) and the sign of its greatness and the pride of its essence and structure.

---

[13] Juristic leadership in the absence of the Imam

We ask Allah the Exalted, the Blessed, for the happy outcome for all serving the Chief of Martyrs (a) and to make us distinguished by the intercession of Hussain (a) in this world and the at the Day of Resurrection.

Thank is due to the Lord of the Worlds and prayers and peace be on our Master Mohammad and his pure progeny (a).[14]

---

[14] www.najaf.org

The late Sayyid Muhammad al-Shirazi's advice about Time Management

"A person's time is extremely limited, so if someone is not careful with how they use their time then the fruits of their actions will be extremely little. The opposite is also true, if someone is careful on their time management and spreads it out amongst their different tasks, and on things they should be implementing in limited time, then they come up with results that almost resemble miracles.

So, it upon the scholar to spread out his time well and with coordination and put for each segment of time a goal they want to accomplish. Time for writing, time for fulfilling the needs of people and their issues, time for institutions, time for congregational prayers, time for the pulpit, time for teaching, and likewise...

And it is also obligatory for him, if he spends his time on something, to spend it on the best aspect of that thing. For example: If he makes specific time for education, he has to see what is the best type of it there is, and start implementing it. If he makes time for visiting people, he should notice that when the people of important positions are visited, end up having the most benefit to those whom visit them, so he should go and visit them. This is the same for every other issue that one has made a specific time slot for."[15]

---

[15] Essence of Insight by Sayyid Muhammad Shirazi

Advice of Ayatollah Sheikh Ishaq Fayyad about Interacting with others 2019

When dealing with people we should deal and interact with them with the best *akhlaq* (morality). This is not just regarding the Muslims, but it is for anyone we interact with regardless of their religion whether they be Shia, Sunni, Christians, Jews or even polytheists.

We must strive to have the best manners just as we find in the example of our noble Prophet (s) who even behaved with the greatest morality even when he was treated badly by others. The Prophet of Islam (s) even treated the polytheists with good manners. We have to be just and fair with people and treat them with good morality just as we find in the example of the Commander of the Faithful Ali (a) when they stole his rights.

We should stay away from falsehood and lying. Falsehood is one of the greatest impurities which Allah has condemned in the Holy Quran. The liar will not be successful in this world nor in the hereafter. We should instead work based on a foundation built upon truthfulness and honesty. We do not want people to see us being as being deceitful or liars then they judge Islam from seeing these corrupt individuals thus forming a bad image of Islam. It is very important for us to always be trustworthy as the Holy Prophet (s) was known as al-Amin (the trustworthy).

We should not backbite others, but rather we should conceal others faults. We should not strive to highlight the faults of others.[16]

---

[16] Relayed by Sheikh Mateen Charbonneau

Advice of Ayatollah Sayyid Murtadha Shirazi about Quality and Quantity- 2019

There are two goals that we should keep in mind: Quality and Quantity.

Quality: We should strive to become people of God, righteous and God-fearing people. People of God can do miraculous things and we can see this by looking at the example of the companions of Prophet Jesus (a). These companions could even walk on water and if they kept getting stronger in their faith they may have even become able to fly! (Hadith)

Righteous individuals such as Salman who have such a high level of faith are *Awliya Allah* (People of God). They have the ability to see the inner workings of people and to see their true nature. They are able to see people for what they really are whether it is as if they are wolves, pigs, dogs, sheep, etc. They see these things yet they do not reveal this knowledge to others.

One time a man came to Imam Sadiq (a) while they were performing Hajj and told the Imam in surprise that look at how many people are performing Hajj. The Imam (a) replied that there is a lot of noise, but the actual amount of people truly performing Hajj is very few.

We should make note that we do not strive to become righteous individuals in order to gain these powers of insight or miracles, but rather we strive to become closer to Allah. These miraculous things are just the outcome of getting closer to Allah but are not the main objective.

We can achieve becoming people of God by removing all things from our hearts other than Allah, cleanse our hearts from the worldly things and filling our hearts with only the love of Allah (swt). We should use the supplication that says: *"O' Allah extract the love of this world from my heart."*

An angel came to the Holy Prophet (s) and presented him two options:

1. To be a King and a Messenger
2. To be a Servant and a Messenger

He chose being a servant and this is even higher than being a king or a messenger. Don't we see that in the *tashahud* of the prayer that we bring servant first when we say: "*Ashhadu anna Muhammadan 'Abduhu wa Rasuluh* (I bear witness that Muhammad is His servant and His Messenger)."

The Awaited Savior Imam Mahdi (aj) is waiting for 313 people of God & true servants of God. Ask yourself what if the number has reached 312? Why can't we be the one who completes the number he is waiting for by being the 313th?

We must purify our heart and mind by not letting them wander right and left. We must work on this matter by solely focusing on Allah in our salat. There is a Shaytan by the name of Khanzab whose specific job is to distract those making salat.

There was a righteous person who used to lead the prayers in the bazaar of Tehran and a lot of people used to pray behind him. On this particular day he started the salat with sincerity then when he reached the line of Surah Fatiha which says *Ihdinas Siratal Mustaqeem* (Guide us to the straight path) he started thinking to himself that he needs a donkey to travel to the masjid of the bazaar, because he is old and the journey is getting difficult. This distracted him until now he realized that he was in the position of bowing (*ruku*).

There was a man praying behind the leader of the salat who was very poor and had old clothes. This man happened to be one of the *Awliya Allah* (Men of God), yet no one knew. When the prayer leader got to that line *Ihdinas Siratal Mustaqeem* this man who was praying in congregation separated himself and prayed the rest of the prayer with a singular intention (*furada*). After he finished, he sat on the ground spread out an old cloth and started eating an old piece of bread and an onion that he had with him.

After everyone else finished the congregational salat they became very upset and started demanding of the man why he did that. He did not want to tell the man publicly, but he kept insisting. So, he said to the prayer leader that once you reached *Ihdinas*... your mind began to wander and you started thinking about buying a donkey. I came to pray behind a righteous man and not someone whose mind is occupied with other things.

This man was sent to warn the prayer leader from letting other things get in the way of him being a righteous man of God. The prayer leader put his face in his hands and started sobbing and when he went to look for the poor man again he was gone.

One of the effective ways to get closer to Allah and also keep the Shaytan away is to prolong our *sujood* (prostration). The Holy Quran says that Shaytan will come to you from the right, left, front and back but it does not mention from above or below. That is because we see that in these directions we raise our hands upwards in qunoot and we place our forehead on the Earth facing down in *sujood*.

When we make our intention to guide others then Allah will bless you to guide yourself. When you strive to guide yourself then Allah will bless you to also guide other people.

Quantity: One of the companions of Imam Sadiq (a) by the name of Jabir ibn Yazid al-Jufi memorized 60,000 narrations of the Imam (a)! We might say that it is impossible to guide a million people, but Allah is the one who guides. We shouldn't cheapen our abilities and set low goals for ourselves. We should set high goals and trust in Allah to aid us. Allah says that He will send rain and He will send sustenance. We have to ask Allah to expand our capacity to be able to hold more knowledge. If we have a small cup it only has the ability to hold a small amount of water for example 8 ounces, but if we have a pitcher then we are able to hold more such as one gallon.

We must prepare ourselves to guide others and to do this we should read the books of successful leaders and study their methods. We must do this in whatever field we choose to go into. For example, we see that the late Ayatollah Sayyid Hassan Shirazi was able to convert two million 'Alawi's to become Twelver Shia's in Syria. We see that some people may write a book and only a few people read it, but then we see that some authors have millions of readers. How did they accomplish this? We must study their methods and see how they were able to get such a successful outcome and we can take from their good methods and use them in order to spread the message of Islam.

We must be persistent in our supplications and also insistent in our asking. We should put our trust in Allah and never lose hope that our supplication will be granted. One of the beneficial supplications to get our needs granted is the abundant saying of: *Mashallah laa quwwata illa billah.*

About being persistent, I remember there was one of the youth who followed my father Ayatollah Sayyid Muhammad Shirazi and at some point he became a communist and left Islam. My father would pass by this youth's shop on his way to salat every day. My father would always say salam to the youth, but the young man would ignore him and never reply. My father kept saying salam to him every day for one year then the youth finally replied to his salam and ended up repenting and coming back to Islam.[17]

---

[17] Relayed by Sheikh Mateen Charbonneau

Advice of Ayatollah Sheikh Ishaq Fayyadh about students of knowledge -2019

The most important thing for the students of knowledge is studying. The student should give his studies priority over other things, so much so that if he is faced with two things such as performing the night prayer (Salat al-Layl) or studying the student should choose studying. This is because the pursuit of knowledge and studying for the student is of the of the upmost importance.[18]

---

[18] Relayed by Sheikh Mateen Charbonneau

Advice of Ayatollah Sayyid Murtadha Shirazi for the Students of Knowledge – 2019

People are in one of these four situations:

1. Present, but absent. For example, some people are present living near the holy shrines of our Imam's (a) yet their minds are absent and they wish they were somewhere else.
2. Absent, but present. For example, someone may be living in a faraway place like America, but their mind and heart is here in Najaf with Amir al Mumineen (a).
3. Present and present. This is meaning they are there in the holy city and they are aware of this bounty and appreciative of it at the same time.
4. Absent and absent. This is meaning that the person is absent from the sacred place near the Imams (a) and also their mind and heart are absent from their Imams (a).

We should always ask Ahl ul Bayt (a) to keep us close to them and not to let our hearts and minds forget them.

We should always keep Allah in mind that He is always present and this thought should prevent us from committing sinful actions.

After every salat we should remember Amir al Mumineen (a) and what he would want from us and that is to aid the religion.

Many times, we think of those who are alive, but we forget about those who have passed on before us. They need our prayers also. The thought of death as a certain reality that we will all face should humble us and keep us away from transgressing.

We must be grateful in all situations and be patient through our hardships. If we are ungrateful to Allah then He will remove our blessings from us.

We read in the narrations that whoever prays under the dome of Imam Hussain (a) will have his need granted. There are also narrations that say wherever the majlis of Imam Hussain (a) is recited becomes a dome, so when you have a need then recite the tragedy of Aba Abdillah Hussain (a) for yourself in your home then supplicate for your needs.

We should carry Sahifa Sajjadiya with ourselves, just as one carries a small pocket-sized Quran. We should read it often and use excerpts from it in our majalis.

Anywhere we are in the world we should strive to be the best and invite others to the path of Ahl ul Bayt (a) by our actions. We have narrations from the Imams (a) that If there are 10,000 and some say 100,000 people in a town and you are not the best of them then you are not from amongst us. We should constantly evaluate ourselves to check for self-improvement especially in the following areas:

1. Increasing our knowledge
2. Taqwa (piety)
3. Morality
4. Good deeds
5. Enjoining the good and forbidding the evil

Shaytan knows our weak points thus we need to realize what they are as well. Just as a country will prepare its military to defend its weak points we must also prepare our army to defend our weak points against our Shaytan.

A very effective dua against the Shaytan is:

اللّهُمَّ إِنَّ إِبْلِيسَ عَبْدٌ مِنْ عَبِيدِكَ يَرانِي مِنْ حَيْثُ لا أَراهُ وَأَنْتَ تَراهُ مِنْ حَيْثُ لايَراكَ وَأَنْتَ أَقْوى عَلى أَمْرِهِ كُلِّهِ وَهُوَ لا يَقْوى عَلى شَيْءٍ مِنْ أَمْرِكَ ، اللّهُمَّ فَأَنَا أَسْتَعِينُ بِكَ عَلَيْهِ يا رَبِّ فَإِنِّي لاطاقَةَ لي بِهِ وَلاحَوْلَ وَلاقُوَّةَ لي عَلَيْهِ إِلاّ بِكَ يا رَبِّ ، اللّهُمَّ إِنْ أَرادَني فَأَرِدْهُ وَإِنْ كادَني فَكِدْهُ وَاكْفِني شَرَّهُ وَاجْعَلْ كَيْدَهُ في نَحْرِهِ ، بِرَحْمَتِكَ يا أَرْحَمَ الرّاحِمينَ وَصَلَّى الله عَلى مُحَمَّدٍ وَآلِهِ الطّاهِرينَ

"O Allah, Iblis (Satan) is one of Your creatures who sees me from a place that I cannot see him and You see him from a place that he cannot see You, and You have power over all his affairs while he does not have power over any of Your affairs. Therefore, O Allah, I resort to You for help against him, because O Lord

(provider, nourisher, sustainer, the one who transforms potentiality into actuality) I do not have any capability against him, no power to change or force to enact, except through You. O Allah, If he intends evil for me, turn it back on him, and if he schemes against me then you scheme against him. Save me from his evil, and make his scheme to attach to his own neck. By Your mercy, O the most merciful of those who show mercy. May Allah bless Muhammad and his purified progeny."

As a student of knowledge one must strive to find out societies weak points and strengthen them. We must be clever in our strategies because people are continuously finding new innovative ways to spread corruption and deviation, so we must also find innovative ways to spread good.[19]

---

[19] Relayed by Sheikh Mateen Charbonneau

Advice from Sheikh Abdul-Karim al-Haeri about Mercy

اَللّٰهُمَّ اجْعَلْ لِي فِيهِ نَصِيباً مِنْ رَحْمَتِكَ الْوَاسِعَةِ، وَاهْدِنِي فِيهِ لِبَرَاهِينِكَ اَلسَّاطِعَةِ، وَخُذْ بِنَاصِيَتِي اِلىٰ مَرْضَاتِكَ الْجَامِعَةِ، بِمَحَبَّتِكَ يَا أَمَلَ الْمُشْتَاقِينَ

O' Allah, on this day, grant me a share from Your limitless mercy, guide me towards Your shining proofs, lead me to Your all-encompassing pleasure by Your love, O the hope of the desirous.

"Truly, the first part of this supplication reminds us of the ever-so eloquent words of Imam Amir al-Momineen (a) in Dua Kumayl where he says: *"O' Allah, I ask You by Your mercy, which embraces everything."*

Also, the Dua taught by Imam al-Sadiq (a) to be recited everyday of Rajab, where it says: *"O' He who gives to one who asks Him. O' He who gives to one who does not ask Him and does not know Him. All out of His compassion and mercy."*

Indeed, the mercy of Allah (swt) knows no boundaries nor limits. Its very nature remains unfathomable in our minds. His mercy encompasses everything. Even those who do not seek Him and implore Him, Allah still gives them their needs and fulfills their request because of His unimaginable mercy. The mercy of Allah is found in the essence of any person's inherent nature. For instance, the mercy of Allah exists in the hearts of the parents who display compassion upon their children. Another example would be believing brothers helping each other out. The list of examples continues. Indeed, all these extend from the overarching mercy of Allah (swt) that is found in every creature.

The nature of Allah's mercy is something that cannot be described; it is truly inexpressible. There are many instances in our holy narrations that allude how in this worldly life, only a small fraction equaling to 1% of Allah's mercy is implemented. On the other hand, the entirety of Allah's mercy will be displayed to the masses in the hereafter. But how can we achieve and be honored by receiving this divine mercy? It is through being merciful and compassionate towards others. It is only then that we deserve attaining Allah's mercy.

To put this into perspective, suppose a friend lent you some money after you had asked. In return, you will repay the exact amount that the person lent you. Of course, you will not give them more money, even though they've done you a huge favor in lending that money. However, when it comes to Allah (swt), it is fundamentally different. This is articulated beautifully in the following verse of the Quran: *"Whoever comes [on the day of Judgment] with a good deed will have ten times the like thereof [to his credit] ...."*[20]

For doing one good action, you will receive ten times the reward from Allah! Many instances like these are found in the Quran. In another beautiful verse, it states: *"The example of those who spend in the way of Allah is just like a grain that produced seven ears, each ear having hundred grains, and Allah multiples [the rewards] for whom He wills."*[21]

It is like committing one good deed that led to the formation of seven ears (ie crops) with each ear having the rewards of 100 grains (deeds), and Allah will multiply that for whom He wills. Not only will the reward be 700 times than it already is, but it can be multiplied to get more rewards! Only one good deed results in that. Now imagine the number of

---

[20] Quran 6:160
[21] Quran 2:261

rewards you receive when you are persistent in these actions!

Therefore, with showing mercy towards a human being, Allah will show you mercy that your mind cannot even begin to imagine its implementation. This is not only limited to humans, but any creature in general.

In a very popular story narrated by the Holy Prophet (s), where he was sitting with a few of his companions, he informed them of an adulteress woman who entered heaven! His companions asked more about this story, so the Prophet (s) further elaborated. He explained that one day, as she was walking by a deserted land, she saw a thirsty dog circling a water well. The lady ripped a portion of her clothes, descended it to the water well to make it wet, and squeezed out the water so that the dog could drink water. For this action alone, she was forgiven for her actions. It was only because she showed a little bit of mercy towards another creation of Allah! Ponder upon this story. A woman who lived a life full of sin was forgiven for performing this action! What about us who constantly aim to please Allah (swt)!

Verily, the mercy of Allah (swt) is great, all-encompassing and cannot be articulated. It is of crucial matter to seek to the best of your ability to attain the mercy of Allah (swt) during this month of Ramadan by doing constant remembrance of God and seeking forgiveness. Only a fool would waste such an opportunity, such as the Holy Month of Ramadan, and not spend the time to seek closeness to Allah to attain His pleasure and mercy!

Consider the following narration. In the Tafsir of the following verse: *"And thus did We show Abraham the realm of the heavens and the earth that he would be among those certain in faith."*[22]

It was narrated that Imam al-Sadiq (a) said: *"When Ibrahim (a) was shown the realm of the heavens of the earth, he witnessed a man committing adultery. Ibrahim (a) then made Dua against him and the man died as a result. He then saw another man do the same act, so Ibrahim made Dua against him and that man died as a result. He then saw three other people commit the same act. Ibrahim (a) made Dua against them and they died as a result. Allah (swt) then sent a revelation to Ibrahim (a) saying: "O' Ibrahim, indeed your Dua's are answered. Do not pray against My servants, for if I wished, I would not have created them. I have created people of three kinds: one who worships Me without ascribing partners to Me, whom I will reward. One who worships other than Me, who I will not forget. And one who worships other than Me, but I will place an offspring from his loins who will worship Me."*[23]

---

[22] Quran 6:75
[23] Tafsir al-Ayashi, volume 1, page 364.

How astonishing! The mercy and forgiveness of Allah even stopped Ibrahim from making Dua's against sinners for the chance that they may repent and attempt to seek proximity to Allah. This is truly forgiveness and mercy which cannot be found except with the one true God!" [24]

---

[24] An Exegesis on The Daily Supplications of The Holy Month of Ramadan by Sheikh Abdul-Karim al-Haeri pg 52-55

Advice from Ayatollah Sayyid Muhammad Ridha Shirazi about Participating in the Rituals of Imam Hussain (a)

"Among the questions that we often ask ourselves is: what is our obligation toward the Master of the Martyrs Imam Hussain (a), His noble household and his loyal companions? Inshallah, we shall address several of these obligations, which are considered amongst the easy obligations.

The great sacrifices and actions were performed by our forefathers. Some of them were beheaded; others had their hands and legs chopped off; others were hanged, and yet they stopped at no limit for the sake of Imam Hussain (a) and his tragedies.

There are some individuals that have boundaries when dealing with Almighty Allah, Prophet Mohammad (s) and his Household (a). They act within these boundaries. However, those (our forefathers)

did not place any limits for their relationship with Imam Hussain (a) and endured great hardships and struggles. Therefore, as we stated, the deeds and obligations that we will discuss will be among the easier of the deeds and obligations.

The first obligation is the financial participation. Regardless of our financial capability (wealthy or poor), each one of us should dedicate a percentage of his wealth that he will share with Imam Hussain (a). It can be 1% or 10 % or 20%. According to what some scholars have told me, certain individuals pay their *Khums* twice per year. They pay the first 20%, as part of their yearly religious obligation for the sake of Allah. They pay the second 20% for the sake of Imam Hussain (a). Ultimately, those individuals pay a sum of 40% of their yearly savings.

Generally, and as far as what I recall, the notion of financial participation was introduced and taught by Imam Al-Sadiq (a).

The story is as follows: Imam Al-Sadiq (a) was on a journey along with a group of people, and some of those travelling with the Imam were carrying money with them. During those days, the majority of roads were not safe, as thieves often ambushed and attacked caravans and travelers and took anything they found with them. In some cases, the travelers were even murdered.

Those individuals travelling with money, said to Imam Al-Sadiq (a): We are afraid of the thieves that might appear in our way. We want to leave our money with you.

The Imam (a) rejected and said: Maybe those looters will attack me as well and take the money.

They replied: Then we shall bury our money somewhere.

Imam Al-Sadiq (a) told those men: But it's possible that someone might come and dig up the money, or you may lose track of where you buried it, when you return to it, and in both cases you will lose your money.

The men asked: Then what should we do?

Imam Al-Sadiq (a) replied: deposit and entrust your money with the one who never loses any deposit or trust.

They asked: And who may that be?

Imam replied: Allah. Lord of the worlds.

They asked: How do we entrust our money with Him?

The Imam (a) replied: By paying 1/3 of your money to the poor.

They asked: How do we pay 1/3 while there are no poor among us?

The Imam (a) said: Intend that if you pass this road safely and arrive to your destination unharmed, you shall pay 1/3 of your money to the poor.

All those men made that intention. During their way, they witnessed the thieves approaching. They were very afraid and asked the Imam (a): The looters are approaching. What shall we do?

The Imam (a) replied: How can you be afraid while you are under the protection of Allah, Lord of the Worlds? There should be no fear.

The thieves approached the caravan, got off their horses and approached the Imam (a) and kissed his hand.

One of them told the Imam (a): We saw the Holy Prophet (s) in our dreams and he ordered us to be at your service. So here we are at your service, and if you want us to deter other looters from your caravan, we shall accompany you.

The Imam (a) replied: There is no need. The One (Allah), who deterred you from harming us, will deter others as well.

They arrived to their destination and those men paid 1/3 of their money to the poor. According to the hadith, those men later profited 10 dirhams for every dirham they gave to the poor.

Our point from this story is revealed in this sentence by Imam Al-Sadiq (a): *You have witnessed the blessings of doing business with Allah. Hence continue on that course.*

Let this be our approach in life. In addition to the obligatory dues, dedicate a specific percentage of your wealth purely for the sake of Allah. This is very important, and it will result in many blessings, as Imam Al-Sadiq (a) stated: *You have witnessed the blessings of doing business with Allah.* Doing business with Allah has blessings. Doing business with Imam Hussain (a) has blessings.

My maternal grandfather was once stuck in a very complicated business deal. Apparently, there was no hope for that business deal to succeed, and he had no way out of the deal. My grandfather turned to Allah and pledged to Abul Fadhl Al-Abbas (a) or to Imam Hussain (a), or to both of them that he would dedicate 1/3 of his entire wealth to them if he were relieved from that predicament.

Fortunately, through the help of Allah, my grandfather was able to get out of that hardship and he fulfilled his pledge until the last day of his life. Any money he would earn, he would dedicate 1/3 of it to them.

This was the first obligation. The financial participation. Each one of us should contribute financially to Imam Hussain (a), even if it's a small amount, such as 1%. That 1% would bring blessings and mercy.

The second obligation is participation with children. One can vow one or more of his children to be a servant for Imam Hussain (a). This child may become a defender of Shia Islam in the world. Don't belittle the importance of that child. This was the second obligation.

A man narrates that when he was a child (8 years old or younger) he saw my late father (Ayatollah Sayed Mohammad Al-Shirazi) on a certain occasion. He tells me: I was a child and your father asked me about my name. I told him my name.

Your father then said: Do you know that one of our great scholars shares your name? This great scholar wrote an outstanding book in several volumes. You should try to become like that great scholar.

The man says: Those words stayed in my mind during my childhood and influenced me greatly.

Don't say he's only a child. The men who are governing the world today, weren't they children at one time? A single world can be so influential.

That child has now grown to be one of the greatest Shia speakers in the world. A motivated child may one day become a defender of Shia Islam around the world. This was the second obligation.

The first obligation was financial obligation. The second obligation was participation with children. The third obligation is personal participation. That means one would personally participate in anything that relates to Imam Hussain (a), through a variety of ways. This personal participation can be done through different forms.

As we mentioned before, we should not place limits for our relationship with Imam Hussain (a). For instance, a personal participation can be as simple as reciting *Ziyarat Ashura*. That's one way to personally interact and participate with Imam Hussain (a) and his cause.

A while ago, a young man from another country was telling me a story. On the Day of Judgment we may envy these individuals. He said that his mother would always recite *Ziyarat Ashura*, and for 30 years she never missed a day. For 30 years this woman had been reciting Ziyarat Ashura every day.

The young man says: A few years ago, my mother decided to travel to Mashhad during the days of Muharram. She travelled to Mashhad during those days, and she died on the tenth day of Muharram, and was buried in the shrine of Imam Al-Ridha (a) in Mashhad.

This example might be presented before us on Judgement Day, where some of us might have never even read Ziyarat Ashura once in their lives.

Wouldn't we envy this woman for her status?

These are all examples of the personal participation with Imam Hussain (a).

I was also informed of another woman that has been reciting Ziyarat Ashura for the past 20 or 10 years. This woman recites Ziyarat Ashura twice a day. Why twice a day?

She says: I want to recite a ziyarat for each day of my life from the moment of my birth. Meaning, she is reading the Ziyarat twice daily to make up for the days that she did not read Ziyarat Ashura. This is another example.

The third example: The story is about one of the merchants that I personally know, who resides in another country. An individual who knows this merchant as well told me: Each day, when this merchant comes to open his store, he walks around a nearby field and recites Ziyarat Ashura. After reciting the Ziyarat, this merchant goes and opens his store.

It is also said that this merchant wakes up daily 2 hours prior to Morning Prayer and prays Salat Al-Layl as well.

He is only a merchant, not a scholar, and he grew up in a very ordinary environment. On the Day of Judgement this merchant and some of us will be summoned, and most likely we will envy his status in the Hereafter.

Participation and interaction in all forms and without limitations, as we mentioned. Meaning, a person should not set a specific limit and boundary for himself when it comes to serving and working for Imam Hussain (a). A person should not place specific considerations before his service for Imam Hussain (a).

As witnessed, when people get older, they start placing limits and boundaries for themselves. Sheikh Al-Wahid Al-Khorasani would say: Many of our great scholars would rely on a *fatwa* if it had consensus among 3 scholars, and they would issue their opinion according to that fatwa as well.

Meaning that based on that consensus they would be assured that there is credible evidence for that religious ruling, since those three scholars were precise and pious.

Those three great scholars were: The Great Sheikh Al-Ansari (A prominent 18th century Shia scholar), The Great Mirza Al-Shirazi (Prominent 18th century Shia scholar and leader of Iran's Tobacco revolution) and Mirza Taqi Al-Shirazi (A prominent 19-20th century Shia scholar, who led the revolution against British occupation in Iraq).

If those three scholars would agree on a specific religious ruling, other great scholars would issue their fatwas and rulings according to theirs.

As you are aware, Mirzi Mohammad Taqi Al-Shirazi was the supreme religious authority for Shia Muslims and led one of the greatest revolutions in history. So, he was both a religious and political leader. Yet, the Mirza would do something on the 10th day of Muharram that most of us might not be willing to do. Mirza would come out of his house on the Day of Ashura barefoot and bareheaded and walk with mourners of Imam Hussain (a) and beat his chest.

Sheikh Al-Wahid would say: This (Mirza's action on the Day of Ashura) was due to his extensive knowledge.

Mirza Taqi Al-Shirazi would see the Hadith of Imam Al-Ridha (a) about His great Grandfather, Imam Hussain (a): *"The day (Ashura) of Hussain has injured our eyelids, and brought down our tears"*

The eye is the most or among the most sensitive and delicate body parts. Hence, how much would someone have to cry in order for his eyelids to be injured? I still have not seen or witnessed anyone, whose eyelids were injured due to excessive crying. Imam Al-Ridha (a) says: *"The day (Ashura) of Hussain has injured our eyelids"*

This is a personal note: We read in Ziyarat Al-Nahiya, Imam Al-Mahdi (aj) says, *"I will lament you every morning and evening, and will weep blood instead of tears."*

As far as I remember, I have not seen anyone cry blood due to excessive crying.

Therefore, Sheikh Al-Wahid states, this (Mirza Taqi's action on day of Ashura) is a sign of his extensive knowledge.

It is not strange for great scholars like Mirza Taqi Al-Shirazi to walk bareheaded and barefoot on the day of Ashura, if Imam Al-Ridha (a) says: *"The Day of Hussain has injured our eyelids."*

A similar story is narrated about Sayed Mahdi Bahr Al-Ulum. (A prominent 18th century Shia scholar). It is said that Bahr Al-Ulum accompanied his students in Karbala on the Day of Ashura to welcome the famous *Towarij* March. (Towarij March is a historic march by mourners from the town of Towarij 20 km outside of Karbala to the Shrine of Imam Hussain (a) on the Day of Ashura).

All of the sudden Bahr Al-Ulum threw his turban, his cane and cloak and started marching with the people and beating his chest.

The students accompanying Bahr Al-Ulum tried to prevent him and told him such a scene is not appropriate for a great scholar.

Bahr Al-Ulum firmly rejected and joined the marchers. Thereafter, the students also joined the march.

Later, some of the close companions of Bahr Al-Ulum asked him about the reason behind his action. He replied: How can I refrain when I witnessed Imam Al-Mahdi (aj) bareheaded and bare-foot with those marchers? Hence, if Imam Al-Mahdi (aj) participates in such rituals and programs, what would our excuse be for not participating?

As said, we should not place a limit and say: I will participate till that limit only. Out participation should be limitless.

My uncle (may Allah prolong his life) says: I have witnessed several great Grand Ayatollahs participating in *Towarij* March on the Day of Ashura. They were part of that march, or as my uncle clarifies, he says: They were jogging in that march with everyone else.

Al-Sayyid Al-Rajaie (May Allah prolong his life) says: There was a very poor man who held a special program on the Day of Ashura. He would hold a majlis for Imam Hussain (a) and then serve food, although it was financially very difficult for him to do so. Later it was revealed that this man would make up an entire year's missed prayers and fasts of deceased people to earn some money, and then spent the money collected from such a hard job to cover the expenses of his program on the Day of Ashura.

Therefore, one should not place any limit for his service to Imam Hussain (a). Inshallah, all of those deeds and services will benefit us in our Hereafter. Any sort of negligence in this aspect will lead to regret on a day where neither wealth nor progeny will be useful. (Day of Judgement)

We will conclude with this story:

It is said, there was a man who had the honor of meeting with Imam Al-Mahdi (aj). Two stories are reported about this man, and my point is within the second story.

It is said that Imam Al-Mahdi (aj) asked this man once: What would happen to you, if you were not able to meet me?

The man replied: My master, I would die, if I were not able to meet with you.

There is an Arabic verbum that says: *A bereaved mother is not like someone hired to cry.*

How would a woman who has lost her child weep? She weeps from the bottom of her heart. She screams. She might even lose her senses temporarily. It was a norm in some countries that groups of women would be paid to weep for the deceased. Would the cries of those hired women be the same as the cries of those close and dear to the deceased? It's nothing more than acting and pretending to cry.

Often, I think that our prayer for Imam Al-Mahdi (aj) is like the prayer and cries of those hired women. It is only words that we utter. "O' Allah hasten the return of our Imam", yet our mind is somewhere else.

However, if we were in Mina during the fire, I don't know, have you heard about the fire in Mina a few years ago? The fire surrounded Mina, and the blaze was burning the tents. How would we pray for ourselves during that situation? I witnessed this, as I was in Mina during the fire. The tents were caught on fire, and we fled to the mountain. I was watching the view from the mountain. The view of those fleeing the fire.

How would you feel during an earthquake? I was in Tehran a couple of months ago, and a minor earthquake struck the outskirts of Tehran. How do we pray during those moments? But when we pray for our Imam (a) and say: "O' Allah hasten the return of our Imam", we say it as a task that we just want to get over with. There is much difference between the two prayers.

This man replied to Imam Al-Mahdi (aj): My master, I would die, if I were not able to meet with you.

Great love can kill the lover at times. *Quranic verse: "But those who believe are stronger in love for Allah."*

Love to us is nothing more than a notion, and we don't really feel it. There is a huge difference between the two. When you think about an ill person, you don't feel his pain. His sickness is just a notion in our minds. However, when we become sick, we feel the pain. There's a difference between the two.

My master, I would die, if I were not able to meet with you.

The Imam (a) replied to him: For that reason, you see us and meet with us.

Due to this love and devotion, the man was able to meet the Imam of his time, Imam Al-Mahdi (aj).

I narrated the first story, as an introduction for the second story about this man.

This man was asked: What were the initial steps that enabled you to eventually see Imam Al-Mahdi (aj)?

He replied: I saw the Holy Prophet (s) in a dream once and told him, O' Messenger of Allah, I want to meet your grandson Imam Al-Mahdi (aj). I want to receive this honor. What is the path to this honor?

The Holy Prophet (s) answered: Weep for my son Hussain (a) twice daily.

The man says: I started doing that.

It is very easy. One can play a tape daily in his house and listen to the tragedies of Imam Hussain (a).

He continues: I persisted on what Prophet Muhammad (s) told me for a year, and after that one year, I had the great honor to meet Imam Al-Mahdi (aj).

We recite in Ziyara Al-Nahiya: *"I will lament you every morning and evening and will weep blood instead of tears"*.

I might have mentioned this before, a scholar posed this question: Would it be recommended based on this statement to weep for Imam Hussain (a) each morning and evening, to follow the example of Imam Al-Mahdi (aj)?

He would present this question (in his discussion). Perhaps the correct answer is yes, since Ahl ul Bayt (a) are our role models. Even saying a small phrase to mourn Imam Hussain (a) like *"O' Hussain"* every morning or evening would be enough.

The obligations we mentioned in this discussion are very easy obligations, compared to the sacrifices our forefathers made.

This is a famous story that many speakers narrate. There was a man on his way to visit the shrine of Imam Hussain (a). During the time of Abbasid Caliph *Al-Motawakkil*, those that visited the grave of Imam Hussain would have their hand cut off by the government.

The man was arrested and told to present his right hand to be cut.

The man presented his left hand.

They asked: why don't you present your right hand?

The man replied: Because you amputated my right hand last year.

These are three easy obligations toward Imam Hussain (a).

The first obligation is the financial participation.

The second obligation is participation through children.

The third obligation is personal participation in various forms and methods of participation and without any limits.

We ask the Almighty Allah to grant us success for such a task. Praise and exaltation be upon the Holy Prophet (s) and his purified household (a)."[25]

---

[25] From the book: Advice from Ayatollah Sayyid Muhammad Ridha Shirazi

Advice of Ayatollah Sayyid Sadiq Shirazi about hope, decision making and facing problems

"Never lose hope or despair, but rather always have hope. Have hope that there will be a way. It might take some time, but you will find it by the help of Allah.

Never be undecided. Sometimes we have decisions in front of us to pick from one thing or the other thing and when we are in this situation we should not remain undecided, but research and take advice from others about the options and then make your decision. Don't waste your time being undecided.

Don't run away from difficulties or challenges. We will not be free from problems. We should face our problems and strive to solve them. This will cause us to grow and develop spiritually."[26]

---

[26] Advice relayed by Sheikh Mustafa Akhound

Made in the USA
Columbia, SC
02 October 2024